D1488718

WRITERS AND THEIR WORK: NO. 156

Thomas Love Peacock

by

J. I. M. STEWART

Published for The British Council
and The National Book League
by Longmans, Green & Co.

Two shillings and sixpence net

'Peacock is one of our greatest creators of the fantastic. And here was the fantastic created for him by God.' So the essayist refers to the Memoirs of Shelley which appeared in Fraser's Magazine, and earlier he reminds us that Peacock's *Four Ages of Poetry* 'provoked the writing of Shelley's famous *Defence*'. Shelley was his friend, Meredith, his son-in-law, and Coleridge his butt in the satires which have made him immortal as the critic of romanticism, and a very typical English bureaucrat of the old school before the days of competitive examinations which he attacked so vigorously in *Gryll Grange*. Peacock has for us an agreeable period flavour, and occasionally his period serves the present time: 'I almost think it is the ultimate destiny of science to exterminate the human race.'

The essayist is the author of the 20th-century volume of the Oxford History of English Literature soon to be published, and of the essay on *James Joyce* in this series. He is a Student of Christ Church, and enjoys a separate reputation as Michael Innes, the writer of detective fiction.

Bibliographical Series
of Supplements to 'British Book News'
on Writers and their Work

GENERAL EDITOR
Bonamy Dobrée

¶ THOMAS LOVE PEACOCK was born at Weymouth on 18 October 1785. He died at Halliford, Middlesex on 23 January 1866.

THOMAS LOVE PEACOCK
*from a portrait by H. Wallis, dated 1858,
in the National Portrait Gallery*

THOMAS LOVE PEACOCK

by

J. I. M. STEWART

PUBLISHED FOR
THE BRITISH COUNCIL
and the NATIONAL BOOK LEAGUE
by LONGMANS, GREEN & CO.

99330

LONGMANS, GREEN & CO. LTD.,
48 Grosvenor Street, London, W.1.
Railway Crescent, Croydon, Victoria, Australia
Auckland, Kingston (Jamaica), Lahore, Nairobi

LONGMANS SOUTHERN AFRICA (PTY) LTD.
Thibault House, Thibault Square, Cape Town,
Johannesburg, Salisbury

LONGMANS OF NIGERIA LTD.
W.R. Industrial Estate, Ikeja

LONGMANS OF GHANA LTD.
Industrial Estate, Ring Road South, Accra

LONGMANS GREEN (FAR EAST) LTD.
443 Lockhart Road, Hong Kong

LONGMANS OF MALAYA LTD.
44 Jalan Ampang, Kuala Lumpur

ORIENT LONGMANS LTD.
Calcutta, Bombay, Madras
Delhi, Hyderabad, Dacca

LONGMANS CANADA LTD.
137 Bond Street, Toronto 2

First Published in 1963
© J. I. M. Stewart, 1963

Printed in Great Britain by
F. Mildner & Sons, London, E.C.1

THOMAS LOVE PEACOCK

I

THOMAS LOVE PEACOCK was born in 1785, the only child of a prosperous London glass merchant, Samuel Peacock, who so far disobliged the infant as to have him baptized in the Scotch Kirk, London Wall, thereby lending some colour to the damaging conjecture that the future satirist's ancestry lay north of the Tweed. Three years later, Samuel Peacock died. But this time he behaved handsomely enough, since he left his widow and child in a pleasant financial independence. They retired to Chertsey—an agreeable Thames-side village some twenty miles up river from London—and to the society of Mrs. Peacock's father, a retired naval officer who had served under Lord Rodney. Mrs. Peacock was a cultivated woman, who composed verse and read Gibbon. Captain Love had lost a leg in the West Indies, but it may be presumed that he moved easily in polite society nevertheless. The boy had thus the good fortune to shed his mercantile background at a tender age, while retaining its material fruits into maturity.

Mrs. Peacock seems to have followed her favourite historian in setting no great store upon formal education. Peacock attended a private school only into his thirteenth year, thereafter making what appears to have been a more or less formal gesture in the direction of commercial pursuits. But this quickly faded out; he had acquired at least the rudiments of Latin and Greek; and on the strength of this armoury he proceeded to educate himself upon his own whim, whether agreeably in his mother's house or equally agreeably in the reading-room of the British Museum. Had he shown any disposition to enter either university, the matter would presumably have been arranged for him. He suggests himself as a youth with some skill in getting just what he wanted—and all he wanted for some years was books, rural surroundings, small expeditions within England and Scotland, a few friendships or acquaintanceships of not too demanding a sort, and the affection and support of his mother. He was twenty-two before he wanted something that he failed to get. This was a girl called Fanny Falkner who, having been snatched from his advances and hastily married to another, died within the year.

> Frail as thy love, the flowers were dead
> > Ere yet the evening sun was set;
> But years shall see the cypress spread,
> > Immutable as my regret.

When Peacock wrote these verses shortly after Miss Falkner's death, 'regret' was a rather stronger word than it has since become. It could consume like fire—and for Tennyson, still, the days that are no more could be wild with it. And Peacock's regret was in a sense immutable, for this girl returned to his dreams in the last weeks of his life. Yet he was a mother's son. He may have lost Fanny Falkner, as his lifelong butt Coleridge lost Mary Evans, because his nature offered no unimpeded road to passionate love. At least he seems to have felt that distraction was required, since he now took the only positive step in the direction of discomfort recorded of him—this by way of having himself appointed secretary to Sir Home Riggs Popham, in H.M.S. *Venerable*. Finding himself, as a result, on board a 'floating inferno'—and thus amid conditions little conducive to the composition of a comedy he had been meditating—he withdrew precipitately, and, instead of being carried off by Sir Home to the Amazon or the Limpopo, spent the summer of 1809 in the more judicious pursuit of the source of the Thames. In the following year he published a poem celebrating the genius of this homely river. He had already published two metrical exercises: *The Monks of St. Mark* and *Palmyra*. He believed himself to be at least a minor poet. But he was a youth of the strongest good sense, and even this modest persuasion was scarcely to survive his meeting a major one. This major poet was Shelley. And Shelley's was the major influence upon Peacock's whole career.

Peacock before meeting Shelley is a little like Coleridge before meeting Wordsworth; there is the same spectacle of an immature talent groping uncertainly amid irreconcileable attitudes. He had just published *The Philosophy of Melancholy*, which is not unlike the worst of Coleridge's early verse: degenerately Augustan in form, inchoately Romantic in substance. Yet the effect of the meeting was not like that attending Wordsworth's and Coleridge's alliance. For it is clear that Shelley quickly became established in Peacock's mind as a fascinating antitype of himself. Here in Shelley was enthusiasm, and here in Shelley's circle was absurdity. And Peacock reacted to these things, not as the simple Romantic whom he had hitherto been inclined to personate, but as one whose complex affinities lay as much with Addison and Goldsmith as with the leaders of the Revival. He looked at Shelley—the twenty year-old Shelley of the Bracknell period—and loved him. He looked at him again, looked at his companions, like Matthew Arnold murmured 'What a set!'—and upon that murmur the satirist Peacock was born. Yet the love survived, and the Romantic in him survived as well. That is why Peacock is as good a satirist as he is.

Consider his account of the Bracknell coterie:

> At Bracknell, Shelley was surrounded by a numerous society, all in a great measure of his own opinions in relation to religion and politics, and the larger proportion of them in relation to vegetable diet. But they wore their rue with a difference. Every one of them adopting some of the articles of the faith of their general church, had each nevertheless some predominant crotchet of his or her own, which left a number of open questions for earnest and not always temperate discussion. I was sometimes irreverent enough to laugh at the fervour with which opinions utterly unconducive to any practical result were battled for as matters of the highest importance to the well-being of mankind.

The novelist lurks in this distinguishably enough. So does another Peacock who was in the making. 'Opinions utterly unconducive to any practical result' were delectable to him as a writer, but the voice that censures them here is also the voice of the man who was to rise high in the service of the East India Company. Shelley's circle, and Shelley's difficulties, had their share in creating both these mature Peacocks.

The circle provided some irresistible figures of fun. For example, there was J. F. Newton, whose vegetarian principles were implicated with his great discovery that there were four compartments, as well as two hemispheres, in the ancient Zodiac of Dendera. Peacock, interestingly enough, was not quite impervious to this sort of thing; it appears that he planned, and in part carried out, a poem based on Newton's cosmology. Nursing a fantastic bent of his own, he was capable of a sympathetic as well as a sceptical response to the fantastic in others. Had the balance been a little different here—had it approached, for example, that which was to obtain in W. B. Yeats—something significantly imaginative might have emerged from Peacock's frequentation of a lunatic fringe. What was in fact to emerge was the Mr. Toobad of *Nightmare Abbey*. Not that poetry itself was abandoned at this time. On the contrary, he wrote a good deal of it, including *Rhododaphne*, the most successful of his longer works in verse.

But he was not a poet—and what was growing in him in these years was, in the broadest sense, critical power. The mingling in Shelley of genius and absurdity was a perpetual challenge to analysis. Yet we misrepresent Peacock if we exhibit his part in the relationship as that of a merely detached and amused spectator. Sympathy was again important. His association with Shelley's studies was very close; the two evolved ideas and generated enthusiasms together. Peacock was the older man by seven years; it was his natural rôle to supply a maturer judgement, a moderating influence, as the emotional crises and practical perplexities constituting Shelley's diurnal life came along. Peacock's was not a powerful mind, but it was a mind existing in admirable

balance, and one capable of forming, and rendering persuasive, equitable views. Shelley's matrimonial vagaries
constituted a worthy testing-ground here. Peacock saw and
asserted the merits as well as the limitations of Harriet
Shelley; despite much provocation, he maintained an
equally fair view of Harriet's more intellectual if less attractive supplanter, Mary Godwin. He enters the Shelley period
as something of a dilettante poetaster. He emerges from it
as a man of integrity and judgement, and also as a man of
affairs. When Shelley left for Italy in 1818, Peacock—who
was never to see him again—transacted his London business.
When Shelley was drowned in 1822, Peacock and Lord
Byron became his joint executors.

In 1818 Peacock was still living with his mother in rural
seclusion. It may be that the departure of Shelley persuaded
him to take stock of himself. He was writing a little verse;
he was composing an *Essay on Fashionable Literature*; he was
reading and rambling as usual. The total picture may have
come to him as not that of any sort of genius, as not even that
of a dedicated and professional man of letters. Whether for
this reason or on financial grounds, he now looked for a
berth—but on dry land this time. And he found it in the
service of the East India Company. Interest was doubtless
made for him. But he appears to have been subjected to a
fairly stiff probation, and even to something the hearty
detestation of which was to become one of his ineradicable
crotchets: competitive examination. Nor was his employment any kind of sinecure. He worked with colleagues of
the first ability, including James Mill and John Stuart Mill;
and in the wake of James Mill he rose eventually to a
position of major responsibility. The satirist of the Steam
Intellect Society became, ironically enough, the Company's
chief expert upon steam navigation, and in numerous ways
this convinced opponent of rapid locomotion effectively
speeded up physical communications with India. Shelley,
before he died, was to laugh at Peacock as a powerful
bureaucrat, and at the same time to suggest hopefully that

his friend might secure him interesting employment as a political officer at the court of some rajah. It is amusing to speculate on what might have been the literary consequences of so strange a proposal, had it been carried out.

Bureaucrat or not, Peacock was not quite done with being a romantic—and in the first decades of the nineteenth century it was scarcely possible to support that character on the strength of a familiarity merely with the Cotswolds and the Chilterns. Mountains were essential to any full afflatus, and a mountain was better still if inhabited or frequented by a mountain maid. In 1811 Peacock had had the boldness to make an expedition to Wales. There had been mountains galore, and it had been a great success. Now, in 1819, casting a retrospective glance upon the occasion, he recollected that there had been a mountain maid as well; a certain Jane Gryffydh, a parson's daughter. He had neither seen the lady, nor corresponded with her, since then. Now however— being yet more comfortably provided for than hitherto— he sat down and wrote her a letter, the topic sentence of which is the following:

> The same circumstances which have given me prosperity confine me to London, and to the duties of the department with which the East India Company has entrusted me: yet I can absent myself for a few days once in every year: if you sanction my wishes, with what delight should I employ them in bringing you to my home!

Shelley remarked that here was something very like the *dénouement* of one of Peacock's novels. And we may feel it to be an oddly low-temperature technique in the establishing of a love relationship. Yet—as with a Sylvan Forester and an Anthelia Melincourt—there is no evidence that the marriage which succeeded upon it was unsatisfactory to either party.

Very little that is remarkable attended the long course of Peacock's middle and later life. His family having increased —children being born, his mother continuing to live—he established himself at Lower Halliford, still on the Thames, where he remained for the rest of his days. A lover of Athens and Rome, and a wanderer amid all the literatures to which the Mediterranean basin has given birth, Peacock remained an untravelled hyperborean to the end. It is an index of the extent to which he recognized that the larger world of his literary and historical imagination was an ideal world only. And we have to notice that his convivial world—the Peacockian world—was in some degree that too. He loved actual good talk. He loved actual good food and good wine —taking a hand, without doubt, in his elder daughter Mary's learned yet practical essay on 'Gastronomy and Civilization', and giving careful thought to the ordering of his own dinner and the ritual of his own dinner-table. Yet he moved comparatively little in literary and intellectual, as in any other, society. His family, his garden and his river were enough for him, so that we have little record of him in the memoirs of his younger contemporaries. For a description of him in old age we have to turn to a grand-daughter. After speaking of his wit and epicureanism, she goes on:

> In public business my grandfather was upright and honourable; but as he advanced in years his detestation of anything disagreeable made him simply avoid whatever fretted him, laughing off all sorts of ordinary calls upon his leisure time. His love of ease and kindness of heart made it impossible that he could be actively unkind to any one, but he would not be worried, and just got away from anything that annoyed him. . . . He could not bear any one to be unhappy or uncomfortable about him.

Peacock at least knew very well that care is not to be excluded even from a library or a river-bank or a garden, and in his domestic life he had perhaps more than an average share of worry. His wife's health failed, a favourite daughter died in early childhood, a son was unstable. His eldest daughter, Mary Ellen, widowed as a young woman, married George Meredith, who was nine years her junior, and the couple lived with, and indeed on, Peacock for a number of years. Meredith was a good many things that Peacock disliked: Germanophil for one thing and not quite confidently a gentleman for another. He had moreover the disgusting modern habit of smoking tobacco. In these things there was merely irritation, but the end of the story was tragedy. Mary Ellen ran away with a painter, Henry Wallis, and returned a year later, alone and a dying woman. Meredith was unforgiving and always remained so, declining further dealings with his father-in-law—from whom he had learnt something about food and wine and a great deal about the possibilities of intellectual comedy.

In 1865, when Peacock was 81, a fire broke out in the roof of his bedroom. He withdrew to his study, from which he refused to be moved. The fire was extinguished but the shock had done its work, and Peacock died a few weeks later. Curiously, during his last years, he developed a morbid fear of fire; it seemed the first symptom of an approaching senile dementia. The burnt child fears fire. But so does the man who has declined it, or who has found it decline him. In 1820 the mortal remains of Shelley had been consumed by fire, and in a fitting symbolism, on an Italian beach. Peacock, who had taught Shelley so much good sense, lived on for another forty-six years, incombustible.

II

Headlong Hall was published anonymously in 1815, six months after the Battle of Waterloo. *Mansfield Park* had appeared in the year preceding, and *Emma* was to appear in the year following. The Hundred Days seem as remote from Peacock's world as from Jane Austen's. Yet *Headlong Hall* is, if in a restricted sense, a topical novel; it satirizes contemporary persons and their notions in the sphere of literature, science and philosophy.

All philosophers, who find
Some favourite system to their mind,
In every point to make it fit,
Will force all nature to submit.

The epigraph, which is from Swift, may be taken as announcing the governing idea of all Peacock's conversation novels. And all adopt, broadly, the same method: the drawing together in some generously and heterogeneously hospitable place, typically a country house, of a congeries of characters severally subscribing to every intellectual quirk, oddity and crotchet under the sun. Perhaps because stage comedy affords him a primary model, Peacock starts off by aiming in this kind at a good deal of somewhat unambitious amusement. He throws in characters whose bonnets harbour some one small and monotonously buzzing bee, and who are entertainingly bizarre for a short appearance or two, while being of very limited utility thereafter. Squire Headlong himself falls into this category; we are told that he has been 'seized with a violent passion to be thought a philosopher and a man of taste'; but his part in a speculative discussion is commonly a command to buzz the bottle, eschew heel-taps, and take due note that 'as to skylight, liberty hall'. The incompatibility of the squire and his guests is funny in a limited way, but on the whole he has to be left behind. In inventing him Peacock may have been remembering Johnson's Dick Minim. Or he may simply have hit upon him because he wanted a Welsh setting. He had spied a really piquant incongruity in setting some of his very urban philosophers tramping among the mountains.

From the start Peacock reveals himself as so literary a writer that criticism is tempted to dwell on his sources. Yet from the start his virtues are so idiosyncratic that one feels the tracing of derivations to be of only minor interest. Besides the tradition of stage comedy there is, of course, that of the English eighteenth century novel, from which he derives both an intermittent rough-and-tumble, and the habit of using courtship as a light scaffolding round which to erect anything of greater interest and liveliness that comes along. From French *contes* of the same period he draws the notion of incorporating speculative debate, rendered in finished prose, in fiction. The embodying of opinion—the giving this or that contention not merely a voice but also limbs, clothes, a wig, a valet or comic servant, even a mistress and a rudimentary disposition to action: this is something sufficiently widespread in literature; and in our own it is percurrent from William Langland to Bernard Shaw. It is a kind that can very easily go thin or dry, and it can take several fatal turns. For example, it can drift into the dialogue—into the dialogue with unnecessary trimmings, as it does in the third act of Shaw's *Man and Superman*. Or the characters can come to look forbiddingly like personifications. *Headlong Hall* seems at first reading not at all a subtle performance, and when we find that its principle characters are respectively a perfectibilist, a deteriorationist and a statu-quo-ite we may feel that we are going to get very little flesh and blood. But this is not so. The doings of the people as people may be farcical or otherwise absurd. But the people do go through a sort of bustling course of things more or less congruous with their speculative persuasions; we are just able to maintain a sense of them as enjoying and suffering human beings; as a result, the book has life as fiction. Peacock's thread of connection with the novel proper here announces itself, once for all, as slender enough. But he has the art never to sever it.

Take Mr. Escot, the deteriorationist, who gets the lion's share of the talking in *Headlong Hall*. He is from the start a satisfactory monomaniac largely because he is able to summon so accomplished a rhetoric to the support of his *idée fixe*:

> These improvements, as you call them, appear to me only so many links in the great chain of corruption, which will soon fetter the whole human race in irreparable slavery and incurable wretchedness: your improvements proceed in a simple ratio, while the factitious wants and unnatural appetites they engender proceed in a

compound one; and thus one generation acquires fifty wants, and fifty means of supplying them are invented, which each in its turn engenders two new ones; so that the next generation has a hundred, the next two hundred, the next four hundred, till every human being becomes such a helpless compound of perverted inclinations, that he is altogether at the mercy of external circumstances, loses all independence and singleness of character, and degenerates so rapidly from the primitive dignity of his sylvan origin, that it is scarcely possible to indulge in any other expectation, than that the whole species must at length be exterminated by its own infinite imbecility and vileness.

This has the fulness and dignity, almost even the *gravitas,* of eighteenth century moral prose. There is Johnson behind it. But in front of it, so to speak, is delicious absurdity—for in 'the primitive dignity of his sylvan origin' there already peep out (when we know the books as a whole) the endearing features of Sir Oran Haut-ton from the next novel. Mr. Escot is typical of the chief personages in Peacock in being both cogent and extravagant. He illustrates, as they all do, something that, a little later in the book, Mr. Cranium expects us to take for granted: namely, that 'his own system is of all things the dearest to every man of liberal thinking and a philosophical tendency'. In this irony, indeed, lies the essence of Peacock's comic world. Liberal thinking and a philosophical tendency ought to make us tentative and openminded; but in fact they go along with the furious riding of one particular hobby-horse. These people show an obsessive tenacity which renders them admirable material for the operations of the comic spirit. When, at the end of the story, Mr. Escot has gained the hand of the lovely Cephalis Cranium by bartering for it the skull of Cadwallader, he rashly declares himself to be the happiest man alive. But he quickly recovers, and adds that 'a slight oscillation of good in the instance of a solitary individual' by no means affects the solidity of his opinions concerning the general deterioration of the civilized world. His marriage has not the slightest effect in weaning him from his faith in the wild man of the woods, 'the original, unthinking, un-scientific, unlogical savage'. At the same time, he celebrates that marriage with an eminently thoughtful, scientific and logical speech against the relations of the sexes as civilization orders them. His bride is presumably standing beside him as he orates. Regularly in Peacock there is at least the effective ghost of a dramatic setting. It is not so very far from this to the admirable finale of *Man and Superman*, with Jack Tanner caught but speechifying still, and Ann Whitefield telling him encouragingly to go on talking.

Commentators, looking forward to the manner in which Peacock later developed his art, sometimes assert that Mr. Foster, believing in perfectibility, represents Shelley, and that Mr. Escot, being *laudator temporis acti*, must be Peacock himself. There is not very much in this. Among the characters who carry on a general philosophical debate in *Headlong Hall*, as distinct from those who chatter on minor topics, only one, Mr. Panscope, seems definitely related to a living person, Coleridge. Panscope is the first of a number of Coleridges in Peacock's books: a kind of sighting shot, and a poor one. And one inadequacy would seem to appear at once. Coleridge, if we have at all studied him, comes to us, as does Henry James, pre-eminently as a voice—and here is not the voice we know as Coleridge's. But in this, the presentation is in consonance with Peacock's presentation of all his characters. All speak with the same voice—at least in the sense that Landor's persons do in his *Imaginary Conversations*, or Miss Compton-Burnett's in her novels. Peacock does later find means of rendering, within its embodiment in his own highly characteristic prose, the *movement of mind* of some actual persons. But that is rather a different matter.

There is one other point to be noted about Panscope—small, but of important implication. He has a good tailor and ten thousand a year. It is impossible to tell whether Peacock has simply thrown this in to give Panscope some eligibility as a suitor, or whether he is deliberately making the point that Panscope is *not*, in his personal character,

Samuel Taylor Coleridge. In *Nightmare Abbey*, on the other hand, the Coleridge figure, Mr. Flosky, tells us why he has named his eldest son Emanuel Kant Flosky; and we know that Coleridge had called *his* eldest son Ernest Hartley Coleridge on the same principle of admiration for a philosopher. It is commonly said that Peacock does not bring real people into his books in the way of total caricature or travesty; that he rather takes the publicly professed opinions of real people and infers appropriate imaginary characters from these. This holds only a limited truth. All his novels are, to some extent, *romans-à-clef*, and we can say only that Peacock exercises a good deal of civilized tact in exploiting only lightly the private character of his victims. We cannot say that he didn't 'do' Coleridge again and again so as to make Coleridge appear very absurd, or that he didn't 'do' Southey more than once so as to make Southey appear very despicable.

The satire in *Headlong Hall* is blended with something like impartial debate on serious topics. When Escot sees in the fable of Prometheus 'a symbolic portraiture of that disastrous epoch when man first applied fire to culinary purposes', and when—helping himself to a slice of beef—he goes on to declare that both the Lotophagi and the Hindoos 'depose very strongly in favour of a vegetable regimen', he is delightfully absurd. But when, contemplating what we should think of as the first advances of industrialism, he declares 'by enlarging and complicating your machines, you degrade, not exalt, the human animals you employ to direct them', or when he asserts that the manufacturing system tends 'to multiply factitious desires, to stimulate depraved appetites, to invent unnatural wants, to heap up incense on the shrine of luxury, and accumulate expedients of selfish and ruinous profusion', he is of course the mouthpiece of Peacock and of most thoughtful men from Peacock's day to this. And although it is usually said that in *Headlong Hall*, as not in its successor *Melincourt*, Peacock preserves a sense of open debate and refrains from taking sides, it is surely undeniable that Escot on the whole is allowed to get the better of Foster. Foster, indeed, has an equal power of weighty disquisition; he will call upon us to mark 'the slow, but immense, succession of concatenated intelligence' by which, for example, naval architecture has gradually attained its present state of perfection, or he will effectively oppose to Escot's 'mere animal life of a wild man' the achievement of a civilization which produces a Newton, a Lavoisier or a Locke. But the last words tend to be with his adversary, as here:

'You will allow', said Mr. Foster, as soon as they were again in motion, 'that the wild man of the woods could not transport himself over two hundred miles of forest, with as much facility as one of these vehicles transports you and me through the heart of this cultivated country.'

'I am certain', said Mr. Escot, 'that a wild man can travel an immense distance without fatigue; but what is the advantage of locomotion? The wild man is happy in one spot, and there he remains: the civilized man is wretched in every place he happens to be in, and then congratulates himself on being accommodated with a machine that will whirl him to another, where he will be just as miserable as ever.'

This looks back to Johnson's *Rasselas*, and forward to Matthew Arnold.

Nothing less than human destiny is the theme of the main sequence of debates in *Headlong Hall*. But there are subsidiary topics, two of which stand out. One centres in Mr. Cranium and his science of craniology or phrenology. The other centres in Mr. Milestone and his art of landscape gardening. Mr. Cranium's proposal for the instituting of what would now be called a technique of vocational guidance on the basis of his discoveries is amusing, but we have quickly had enough of him. It is rather different with Mr. Milestone. We can no longer inspect extensive collections of skulls arranged to enforce the truths of phrenology, but we can still visit Blenheim and Stowe, Fountains and Stourhead. The vogue of the Picturesque in its various phases has left its actual impress on the face of England; and its history, moreover, interdigitates with that both of imaginative literature and of the fine arts from the age of Pope to that of Wordsworth. Milestone's main scene, in which he produces his portfolio and shows what he has done for Lord Littlebrain, gains for us, if we have a look at some of the books put out by the improvers, in which an ingenious system of slides, to be drawn back from part of an illustration, gives a 'before and after' view of their activities.

A further point may be made by way of Mr. Milestone. When 'pickaxes and gunpowder, a hanging stove and a poker' are so applied as almost to emancipate the spirit of Mr. Cranium from its terrestrial bondage, he being utterly destitute of natatorial skill and so in imminent danger of final submersion, and so on, we come upon an element of straight slapstick that is to run through all the books. Ludicrous physical mishap has always been a resource of the English novelist. But in defending his use of it, Peacock would probably have appealed to a wider tradition: one including *Hudibras*, Cervantes and Aristophanes. In a much fuller context, the last-named of these is the greatest of his masters, even if at a large remove. One has only to read *The Frogs* to realise this.

III

About a year after the publication of *Headlong Hall* Shelley wrote to Leigh Hunt:

> Peacock is the author of *Headlong Hall*. . . . He is now writing *Melincourt* in the same style, but, as I judge, far superior to *Headlong Hall*. He is an amiable man of great learning, considerable taste, an enemy to every shape of tyranny and superstitious imposture.

There is certainly more of Shelley's influence in the second novel than in the first—and if Shelley had not been a genius he would have been a prig. *Melincourt* is the work of a natural humourist and satirist who has become touched by this priggishness, very much to the detriment of his art. Thus the story's central figure, Sylvan Forester, oscillates between a fantastic creation (which is what he ought to be) and a heavily normative or exemplary one. He is a bore given large scope to be boring in a book that is a good deal longer than is judicious. Yet this last fact is one which we tend to rediscover with surprise upon a fresh reading. Looking back, we have a foreshortened view, recollecting it as being dominated (as it is not) by the superb figure of Sir Oran Haut-ton. The greatest of Peacock's creations is, without doubt, the Seithenyn of *The Misfortunes of Elphin.* But Sir Oran surely comes next. And whereas Seithenyn has a great deal to say for himself, Sir Oran has nothing at all. The Wild Man of the Woods has not got around to articulate speech. He has an air of high fashion, bows grace-fully, takes wine with due ceremony, and plays the flute. He even becomes a member of parliament. But he doesn't speak. The grand characteristic of Peacock's people is, of course, their unquenchable loquacity. And here in the middle of them is Sir Oran, unmistakably the greatest gentleman of the lot. True civilization, we are almost persuaded, would consist in holding our tongue.

The skeleton of *Melincourt* is provided by the common-place formula of the novel of courtship. Anthelia Melincourt is at once an independent heiress, a child of the mountains and an authority on the five great poets of Italy. All this has given her, in the way of love-liking, 'a visionary model of excellence which it was very little likely the modern world could realise'. The modern world tries, sending var-ious suitors to Anthelia's castle, including a wicked nobleman who, upon being rejected, abducts and proposes to ravish her—being prevented in the very act, however, by one of Sir Oran's exercises in supersimian agility. Anthelia then pledges herself to Mr. Forester, who has been making cautious advances to her throughout the book. This courtship must strike us as very stilted and insipid, but it is certainly not meant to appear in a satirical light. Peacock is taking it straight from a variety of the polite fiction of the age to which he cannot have attributed any very significant literary merit, but which he clearly regarded as wholesome and agreeable rather than absurd. What he did indeed judge unwholesome and ridiculous—and pillory again and again— were those (as he conceived them) Germanic romances in which there is a morbid and unnatural confounding of virtue and vice, an exhibiting (as Mr. Flosky has it in *Nightmare Abbey*) of all the 'blackest passions of our nature, tricked out in a masquerade dress of heroism and disappointed benevolence; the whole secret of which lies in forming combinations that contradict all our experience'. So when Mr. Forester congratulates Anthelia on her library—

> You have an admirable library, Miss Melincourt: and I judge from the great number of Italian books, you are justly partial to the poets of that exquisite language. The apartment itself seems singularly adapted to the genius of their poetry, which combines the magnificent simplicity of ancient Greece with the mysterious grandeur of the feudal ages—

when Mr. Forester starts off like this, we are decidedly not being asked to laugh at him. He is speaking out of real literary conviction—Peacock's literary conviction.

Nothing more need be said about the amatory or romantic part of *Melincourt*. We may turn to Sylvan Forester in his other character. He is first encountered as a young gentleman living in affluent retirement (he is the owner of Red Nose Abbey, which he has renamed Redrose Abbey) with a view, he says, 'of carrying on in peace and seclusion some peculiar experiments on the nature and progress of man'. These experiments, in fact, concern Sir Oran, who 'was caught very young in the woods of Angola'. And what Mr. Forester is really proposing is an enormous joke at the expense of the English parliamentary system at its farthest stage

of corruption. He explains this thus to his friend Sir Tele-
graph Paxarett:

> With a view of ensuring him the respect of society, which always
> attends on rank and fortune, I have purchased him a baronetcy, and
> made over to him an estate. I have also purchased of the Duke of
> Rottenburgh one half of the elective franchise vested in the body of
> Mr. Christopher Corporate, the free, fat, and dependent burgess of
> the ancient and honourable borough of Onevote, who returns two
> members to Parliament, one of whom will shortly be Sir Oran.

This wonderful idea affords Peacock scope for a number of
brilliant attacks upon the existing political system, including
some admirable travesties of Canning's speeches against
parliamentary reform, in which *corruption* is pleasantly
softened into *persuasion in a tangible shape*, and in which the
blessings of *virtual representation*, and the arguments gravely
adduced to the effect that the member for a rotten borough
is far more gloriously independent and incorruptible than
the member for a real one, are pilloried with a very sufficient
sparkle of wit. At the actual election, Mr. Corporate appears
and is properly deferred to as *a respectable body of constituents*.
The occasion ends in a riot, and all that in fact exists of the
honourable borough of Onevote (to wit, the hustings and a
marquee: for Onevote has been for centuries a desolate
stretch of heath) is reduced to ashes in a few minutes. All
this is amusing today; it must have been more so in 1817,
when Onevotes, Christopher Corporates, and the blessings
of virtual representation for towns such as Novote, actually
existed and were defended by some of the most astute in-
telligences in the land.

If the high-mindedness of Shelley is responsible for some
of the duller stretches of *Melincourt*, his potentialities as a
figure of fun are the sole prompting occasion of the next,
and much shorter, book, *Nightmare Abbey* (1818). The hard-
worked term *tour de force* is perhaps the aptest that criticism
can find for this performance. Out of Shelley's personality
and intellectual persuasions, and even out of that matrimonial dilemma the resolution of which had been succeeded by

tragedy, Peacock distils an essence which is at once farce and high comedy—and which was to prove entirely acceptable to a victim seldom showing much sense of humour, and very prone to imagine himself the object of malign attack.

Peacock cannot have been unaware of the hazards he ran, yet the book has the appearance of being casually entered upon. Once more there is the country house and the gathering of guests. The house—complete with its towers, moat, owls and dismal fenland setting—is essential; Scythrop Glowry and his father could scarcely exist except against the background it provides. But the collecting within its mouldering walls of a miscellaneous group of cranks is a carry-over from *Headlong Hall* not very well adapted to the higher organisation at which the new book aims. Mr. Asterias the ichthyologist has small function in the story and his son Aquarius has less; nor is Mr. Listless, the fashionable youth who is always listless, an impressive or useful invention. These old elements do not combine well with what is new.

On the other hand, certain others do. *Nightmare Abbey* is still a conversation piece; the passion of all its creatures is to talk; but now there is a situation as well as a dinner-table. The incongruity of the talk and the situation, the absurdity of the characters' continued loquacity in the predicaments in which they find themselves, make the fine irony of the book. Thus when Scythrop retires one evening to his tower in the south-eastern angle of the Abbey he is astonished to find a muffled figure which presently reveals itself as that of a young woman of dazzling grace and beauty. He is much taken aback, and the following exchange ensues:

> 'You are surprised', said the lady; 'yet why should you be surprised? If you had met me in a drawing-room, and I had been introduced to you by an old woman, it would have been a matter of course: can the division of two or three walls, and the absence of an unimportant personage, make the same object essentially different in the perception of a philosopher?'
>
> 'Certainly not', said Scythrop; 'but when any class of objects has habitually presented itself to our perceptions in invariable con-

junction with particular relations, then, on the sudden appearance of
one object of the class divested of those accompaniments, the
essential difference of the relation is, by an involuntary process,
transferred to the object itself, which thus offers itself to our
perceptions with all the strangeness of novelty.'

This is pleasing in itself; it would be so even if we did not
recognize the raillery at the expense of Hartley's sensationa-
list philosophy. Even better are the kindred passages at the
climax, where Scythrop's loquacity is at one and the same
time an endeavour to lead his father off the scent of the
hidden lady and a genuine reflection of his inexpugnably
theoretical mind.

IV

Peacock possessed little resource in drawing out and
diversifying his fable. In *Headlong Hall* the house-party as-
sembles, dines, talks, breakfasts, dines, and so on. Its members
perambulate (or, as Peacock likes to say, perlustrate) the
squire's park; a few of them take slightly longer walks
through the countryside; then they nearly all get married
and—presumably—disperse. In *Nightmare Abbey* the scene
is even more contracted: anybody proceeding beyond hoot-
ing distance of the owls disappears from our ken until he
turns up again; the book is based on a single and simple
comic situation and a variety of conversations, with every-
thing more or less oriented upon the absurdities, and morbid-
ities, as Peacock saw them, of the romantic sensibility.
Melincourt, a much longer book, shows its author in real
difficulty. He adopts a familiar resource of the novelist con-
cerned with keeping going, and sends his characters travelling. But he is no Fielding or Smollett, and the wanderers—
who are supposed to be in urgent quest of a ravished maiden
—simply go on talking as if they were still round a dinner-
table.

In *Crotchet Castle*—the next book (1831) and the chief work of his full maturity—he again tries travelling; this time in a peculiar manner and with more success. The house-party take to house-boats and are drawn up the Thames. They inspect Oxford and its 'undisturbed libraries'. At Lechlade:

> They entered the canal that connects the Thames with the Severn; ascended by many locks: passed, by a tunnel three miles long, through the bowels of Sapperton Hill..; descended by many locks again, through the valley of Stroud into the Severn; continued their navigation into the Ellesmere canal; moored their pinnaces in the Vale of Llangollen by the aqueduct of Pontycysyllty.

This peregrination (which it is still possible to undertake, although soon after Lechlade the canal has become a dry bottom) transports the people of *Crotchet Castle* from one to the other of the only two localities that Peacock much cared for or knew about. The sense of familiar ground makes one of the pleasures of the novel.

But there is more that is familiar about it than that. For the formula is still the same: a host who collects indifferently crackpots and intellectuals, a hero with a stable full of hobby-horses, a heroine who is devoted to books and mountain solitude. But it is all done better than ever before, and the cast, although well-known to us, are almost without exception brilliant in their rôles. Even so, one is pre-eminent. This is the clergyman, Dr. Folliott, whose first entry has something of the splendour of the authentic Shakespearian Pericles in the third act of that imperfectly canonical tragedy:

> 'God bless my soul, sir!' exclaimed the Reverend Doctor Folliott, bursting, one fine May morning, into the breakfast-room at Crotchet Castle, 'I am out of all patience with this march of mind. Here has my house been nearly burned down, by my cook taking it into her head to study hydrostatics, in a sixpenny tract, published by the Steam Intellect Society, and written by a learned friend who is for doing all the world's business as well as his own, and is equally well qualified to handle every branch of human knowledge.'

It is perhaps because in a state of irritation occasioned by this tiresome alarm—conjoined, as it was, with the dubious propinquity to Dr. Folliott's cook of Dr. Folliott's footman —that the Doctor at once falls upon Mr. MacQuedy, a philosopher who has been so rash as to refer to his native Edinburgh as the Modern Athens:

> Modern Athens, sir! The assumption is a personal affront to every man who has a Sophocles in his library. I will thank you for an anchovy.

The Doctor is a Johnsonian bully, perhaps—but there are few instances in which there is not wit in his warfare. *A propos* of the ruling phobia of a certain Mr. Firedamp, he remarks that he himself judges the proximity of wine a matter of much more importance than the longinquity of water. And he finds in praise of education the single circumstance that it gives a fixed direction to stupidity. The eighth chapter of the novel, headed 'Science and Charity', in which he first fustigates a couple of footpads whom he chooses to regard as swearing by the learned friend (who is Lord Brougham), and in which he is later interviewed by Charity Commissioners who solemnly admonish him upon the misappropriation of a shrunken and minute charitable endowment he has never heard of—this at great public expense and without even requiring or suggesting that the pound a year involved should be charitably applied again: this chapter is one of the most amusing in the book. It is perhaps worth notice, as instancing the perfecting of Peacock's art, that it is only among his intimates that Dr. Folliott explodes about all this. To the itinerant Commissioners he behaves with polite restraint. He is, in fact, a rounded character, and his foibles never take him beyond the bounds of good-breeding or away from the gravity proper to his cloth. Even his attitude to the pleasures of the table is in every sense weighty. 'The current of opinion', he says, 'sets in favour of Hock: but I am for Madeira; I do not fancy Hock till I have laid a substratum of Madeira.' And there hovers in his mind as it were the Platonic idea of a fish sauce which, could he but give it actuality, he would christen with the name of his college—thus handing down that college to posterity as a seat of learning indeed.

Peacock's final book, *Gryll Grange* (1860) is a work of old age. It has its novel facets; yet we shall be impatient with it if we are impatient at being rather lavishly offered the mixture as before. In Dr. Opimian there is a milder Dr. Folliott —but one still capable of saying much that is pertinent to us today. 'Science is one thing and wisdom is another', he early remarks. 'Science is an edged tool with which men play like children and cut their own fingers... See how much belongs to the word Explosion alone... I almost think it is the ultimate destiny of science to exterminate the human race.'

Yet Dr. Opimian's philosophy is not exacting. 'Whatever happens in this world', he advises a lovelorn young farmer, 'never let it spoil your dinner'—and this advice he presently sharpens to 'Live in hope, but live on beef and ale'. Generous in denunciation and reactionary in sentiment ('I have no wish', he says, 'to expedite communication with the Americans'), he has yet concluded that there is more good than evil in the world. We are inclined to infer that this is Peacock's conclusion too—and it is scarcely one consonant with much fulness or sharpness of satire. The earlier novels are by a satirist who hangs his satire upon the peg of a love story for want of a better one; here the writer is an old man who likes to think that the young people about him are happy, and who is prompted to present prosperous courtship in rather more detail than hitherto. A good deal of it is tedious, but a little is fresh. Here, at the end of his life, very curiously, there is the ghost of a different sort of novelist haunting Peacock.

Miss Gryll, the squire's niece, has turned down many suitors, and seems hard to please. When the narrative opens, it is upon a new candidate, Lord Curryfin, who is an adherent of the Broughamian Pantopragmatic Society—and who, we are told, 'valued what he learned less for the pleasure which he derived from the acquisition, than from the effect which it enabled him to produce on others'. Lord Curryfin's grand subject is fish, and he has been going round watering-places giving lectures designed alike to please the visiting gentry and to instruct the local fisherman in their business. This is scarcely promising—and indeed it is clear that at the start Lord Curryfin is designed as a merely comic character. But Peacock seems to feel that he should at least be given a fair run for Miss Gryll's hand, and to effect this the young man must be granted a greater degree of eligibility than is represented simply by his being a lord. So he is promptly endowed with a considerable amount of good sense, and a disposition to laugh at pantopragmatics as a youthful folly put behind him. He remains a pantopragmatic in the eagerness with which he takes up whatever project comes along, and he becomes, among other things, the mainstay of the amateur theatrical activity running through the book.

Lord Curryfin's rival, Mr. Falconer, is the most freakish of all Peacock's heroes. Like the poet Yeats after him—but on a much larger scale—he has re-edified a ruined tower. In this he lives with a household of seven young women—not gentlewomen, but with the accomplishments of gentlewomen—who minister to him in the solitary, meditative and mediaevalising life he has designed for himself. He has always placed the *summum bonum* of life in tranquillity, not in excitement, so it is unfortunate that Miss Gryll is one day struck by lightning more or less at his front door, and has to remain for a considerable period in his house, nursed by the seven handmaidens. But it is only when Dr. Opimian marshals seven young farmers prepared to marry Mr. Falconer's entourage that the match becomes feasible. And, even so, we cannot feel that Mr. Falconer's views on courtship are of a kind likely to please a nice girl. He soliloquizes:

> 'It would be more fitting, that whatever I may do should be done calmly, deliberately, philosophically, than suddenly, passionately, impulsively.'

. . . He dined at his usual hour, and his two Hebes alternately filled his own glass with Madeira.

Clearly we are meant to find this amusing. But, equally clearly, we are not meant to dismiss Mr. Falconer from our regard as a young man displeasingly deficient in radical masculinity. And we may conclude that Peacock has not made up his mind whether the kind of wooing here described is exemplary or the reverse. Perhaps we may further conclude that here is a particular instance of something pervasive in Peacock. George Saintsbury speaks of his 'noble disregard of apparent consistency' and of his 'inveterate habit of pillar-to-post joking'. If he is, in a last analysis, supreme as a creator of fun rather than of satire, it is because he is content or constrained to bear a divided mind before a good many important topics. Perhaps all his superficial dogmatism compensates for, as all his quick laughter masks, a fundamental uncertainty of response to life. Perhaps it is so. Or perhaps this is to take too seriously the dissection of one of the most amusing of writers.

V

So much for the conversation novels that have made Peacock famous. *Maid Marian* (1822) and *The Misfortunes of Elphin* (1830) may be styled romantic tales, but they derive their flavour from that ambiguity in Peacock which we have just been considering. His life's work, as the late Humphry House pointed out, can be viewed as the critique of romanticism—yet in regard to the romantic idea he never quite finally knew where his heart lay. Thus, like any romantic from Gray onwards, he was enchanted by mountain scenery, and celebrated it in verse as being likely to conduce to elevated feeling. At the same time there was a detached Peacock (as there was a detached Coleridge) who perceived that this is moonshine; that human beings in the highlands are as indifferently honest as human beings in the lowlands; and that what makes for moderate decency is not the contemplation of falls and cataracts but the reading of 'ancient books'. (Coleridge says the same thing, but names the Bible.) Again, Peacock had nourished his historical imagination not only on the classics but on Welsh legend and Italian poetry. He could read Scott in the spirit of one accepting Spenser's image of antique times; equally he could attack Scott—as he makes Dr. Folliott attack him—as a mere master of pantomime and fancy dress. He thus had ready to hand either of the moralist's ways of exploiting the past. A 'goodly image' can be held up as a touchstone in Spenser's fashion, and it can be maintained that the march of mind has simply resulted in dragging us far beneath it. On the other hand, by showing people of a remote age and superficial strangeness behaving with just the present age's rascality, one can bring that rascality freshly home. *Maid Marian*, which is little more than an episodic rehandling of the Robin Hood stories, with much interspersed verse, owes most of what interest it possesses to a mingling of these methods. At the same time it has a more popular appeal than anything else that Peacock wrote, and it had a long and successful history as an operetta.

The Misfortunes of Elphin, based upon Welsh legendary material, is a similar romantic narrative refracted through the medium now of a simply comic, and now of an ironic, temper. As in *Maid Marian*, there is much laughing satire at the expense of common and perennial human nature as these peep through ancient habiliments—the humour being sufficiently dry to sustain itself vis-à-vis events sometimes violent and brutal rather than funny in themselves. But there is also—at least in one early stretch of the book—a more specific satirical intent in which the quarry is one we have already seen hunted in *Melincourt*, when Sir Oran is elected for Onevote. The felicitousness of the attack on the decay of parliamentary institutions in *The Misfortunes of Elphin* is partly in the way it takes us by surprise. We may be reminded of a character in *Headlong Hall*, who distinguished the quality of *unexpectedness* as important in the laying out of grounds.

In the beginning of the sixth century the kingdom of King Gwythno existed in a state of easy prosperity. Much of it, however, was protected from inundation only by a massy stone wall, the maintenance of which was vested in Prince Seithenyn as Lord High Commissioner of Royal Embankment. He executed his charge

> as a personage so denominated might be expected to do: he drank the profits, and left the embankment to his deputies, who left it to their assistants, who left it to itself.

A conscientious official, Teithrin, draws the attention of the king's son Elphin to the danger. Together they visit Seithenyn and find him in the middle of a carouse; he is first introduced to us as roaring aloud: 'You are welcome all four' and in the ensuing interview he develops a defence of his neglect in terms of a fuddled logic which represents the acme of Peacock's achievement as a humourist:

> 'Decay', said Seithenyn, 'is one thing, and danger is another. Everything that is old must decay. That the embankment is old, I am free to confess; that it is somewhat rotten in parts, I will not altogether deny; that it is any the worse for that, I do most sturdily gainsay. It does its business well: it works well: it keeps out the water from the land, and it lets in the wine upon the High Commission of Embankment. Cupbearer, fill. Our ancestors were wiser than we: they built it in their wisdom; and, if we should be so rash as to try to mend it, we should only mar it.'
>
> 'The stonework', said Teithrin, 'is sapped and mined: the piles are rotten, broken, and dislocated: the flood-gates and sluices are leaky and creaky.'
>
> 'That is the beauty of it', said Seithenyn. 'Some parts of it are rotten, and some parts of it are sound.'
>
> 'It is well', said Elphin, 'that some parts are sound: it were better that all were so.'
>
> 'So I have heard some people say before', said Seithenyn; 'perverse people, blind to venerable antiquity: that very unamiable sort of

> people who are in the habit of indulging their reason. But I say,
> the parts that are rotten give elasticity to those that are sound. . . .
> It is well: it works well: let well alone. Cup-bearer, fill. It was half
> rotten when I was born, and that is a conclusive reason why it
> should be three parts rotten when I die.'

This is very funny in itself. But the point of the satire is
that statesmen were really talking much as Seithenyn talks,
and Peacock indeed is contriving to follow quite closely
actual speeches made in opposition to current proposals for
electoral reform.

VI

Finally, we may consider two of Peacock's non-fictional
works. *The Four Ages of Poetry* (1820) is commonly said to
owe its celebrity to the circumstance that it provoked the
writing of Shelley's famous *Defence*; otherwise, it would
remain in the obscurity attending the small body of Peacock's other minor and occasional writings. Clearly, it is not
wholly serious. Like Maurice Morgann's essay on Falstaff,
indeed, it is best regarded as a kind of poker-faced joke. But
it differs from Morgann's essay in not being disinterested.
Peacock has an axe to grind:

> Mr. Scott digs up the poachers and cattle-stealers of the ancient
> border. Lord Byron cruizes for thieves and pirates on the shores of
> the Morea and among the Greek Islands. Mr. Southey wades through
> ponderous volumes of travels and old chronicles, from which he
> carefully selects all that is false, useless, and absurd, as being essen-
> tially poetical; and when he has a common-place book full of
> monstrosities, strings them into an epic. Mr. Wordsworth picks up
> village legends from old women . . . .

Judged as a critical thesis, *The Four Ages of Poetry* is merely
a concoction for the purpose of depreciating what it calls
'that egregious confraternity of rhymsters, known by the

name of the Lake Poets', and some others as well. Shelley cannot have been worried by all this. Nor can he have failed to see that the general trend of the piece is ironical, so that what Peacock intends is itself a defence of true poetry. But Shelley was presumably sensitive to that ambiguity which we have remarked as fundamental to his friend's mind. The cyclic view of poetry propounded in the essay has very little substance. But there lurks in it—ready to take what weight we please—an argument drawing upon Locke and upon the empirical and utilitarian traditions which followed him: the argument that, in an age of advancing science, the poetic activity must be progressively circumscribed and finally wither away. It was this that roused Shelley and produced his finest venture into prose.

But Shelley might never have been aware of *The Four Ages of Poetry*—and *A Defence of Poetry*, in consequence, might never have been written—had Peacock not been Shelley's friend. To that friendship the principal memorial is the *Memoirs of Shelley*, written forty years after the poet's death, and made up of four separate contributions, variously occasioned, to *Fraser's Magazine* between 1858 and 1862. The first begins with a certain amount of high-minded reluctance to write about the personal life of Shelley at all. There is no doubt that Peacock sincerely detested that sort of public tittle-tattle on the strength of private intimacy which he castigates in *Crotchet Castle* in the character of Mr. Eavesdrop. And his handling of the central point of scandal in Shelley's life is guarded as well as judicious. But when he comes to give his own reminiscences he knows that a superb portrait is within his power, and the temptation is one that he is unable to resist. It would be quite wrong, however, to suggest that he sets the novelist in himself to work. The salient feature of his account is its avoidance of any exaggeration or heightening of effect. Much of it is extremely amusing, but this is achieved entirely without travesty. The Shelley of the *Memoirs* is much madder than Scythrop Glowry is ever depicted as being. But he is at the same time quite, quite real. And one gets a fresh view of the extraordinary tact that went to the creating of Scythrop when one has had a close look at the Shelley whom Peacock knew.

Far more than with Hogg, Medwin, Trelawny or anybody else until the egregiously dull Professor Dowden, we have a feeling that Peacock is a reliable chronicler. When he tells us of Shelley's living 'chiefly on tea and bread and butter, drinking occasionally a sort of spurious lemonade, made of some powder in a box', we may be confident that the spuriousness of the lemonade hasn't been invented by way of good measure. When Shelley, accepting Peacock's prescription, changes his diet to 'three mutton chops, well peppered' and Peacock declares 'the success was obvious and immediate', we need have no hesitation in believing that it was so. And this holds, too, of his rather astonishing account of Shelley's delusions. This is the best part of the *Memoirs*— not so much because of its bizarre character as because of the perfection of tone with which the amusing, yet ominous, spectacle is presented to us. Reading the account of the mysterious incident of Williams in 1816, we may be disposed to doubt whether the maintenance of a cool and rational scepticism was as therapeutic as Peacock in his psychiatric innocence believed. But we cannot doubt that here, and after a long interval of years, is one of the most consummate pieces of reporting in the language. Peacock is one of our greatest creators of the fantastic. And here was the fantastic created for him by God. It is wonderful that he felt no challenge; that he humbly and so perfectly recreated the thing in itself, forty years on.

THOMAS LOVE PEACOCK

A Select Bibliography

(Place of publication London, unless stated otherwise)

Bibliography:
A full-dress bibliography by Dr. E. Nicholas is in active preparation for publication in the Soho Bibliographies.

Collected Editions:
THE WORKS, edited by H. Cole. 3 vols. (1875).
NOVELS, CALIDORE, AND MISCELLANEA, edited by R. Garnett, 10 vols. (1891).
NOVELS AND RHODODAPHNE, edited by G. Saintsbury. 5 vols. (1895-7).
POEMS, edited by R. B. Johnson [1906]
—in the Muses' Library.
PLAYS, edited by A. B. Young (1910).
WORKS, edited by H. F. B. Brett-Smith and C. E. Jones. 10 vols. (1924-34)
—the definitive Halliford editon, with a biographical introduction superseding previous studies, and full bibliographical and textual notes.
THE NOVELS, edited by D. Garnett (1948).

Selections:
SELECTIONS, edited by H. F. B. Brett-Smith (1928).
THE PLEASURES OF PEACOCK, edited by B. R. Redman. New York (1948).

Separate Works:
THE MONKS OF ST. MARK (1804). *Verse.*
PALMYRA, AND OTHER POEMS (1806). *Verse.*
THE GENIUS OF THE THAMES. A LYRICAL POEM IN TWO PARTS (1810). *Verse*
—the edition of 1812 includes *Palmyra, and Other Poems* (1806) and two additional poems.
THE PHILOSOPHY OF MELANCHOLY, A POEM IN FOUR PARTS WITH A MYTHOLOGICAL ODE (1812). *Verse.*
SIR HORNBOOK: OR, CHILDE LAUNCELOT'S EXPEDITION. A GRAMMATICO-ALLEGORICAL BALLAD (1814). *Verse.*
SIR PROTEUS, A SATIRICAL BALLAD (1814). *Verse*
—written under the pseudonym of P. M. Donovan.

HEADLONG HALL (1816). *Novel*
—with a new preface and with three other novels by Peacock in Bentley's Standard Novels series, 1837.
MELINCOURT. 3 vols. (1817). *Novel.*
THE ROUND TABLE, OR, KING ARTHUR'S FEAST [1817]. *Verse.*
RHODODAPHNE: OR THE THESSALIAN SPELL (1818). *Verse.*
THE FOUR AGES OF POETRY (1820). *Criticism*
—edited by H. F. B. Brett-Smith, Oxford, 1921, in the Percy Reprints series.
MAID MARION (1822). *Novel.*
THE MISFORTUNES OF ELPHIN (1829). *Novel.*
CROTCHET CASTLE (1831). *Novel.*
PAPER MONEY LYRICS, AND OTHER POEMS (1837). *Verse*
—privately printed.
MEMOIRS OF PERCY BYSSHE SHELLEY (1858–62). *Memoirs*
—edited by H. F. B. Brett-Smith, 1909, with Shelley's letters to Peacock. See also *Shelley and his Circle* (The Pforzheimer Library), 1961.
GRYLL GRANGE (1861). *Novel.*
INGANNATI: THE DECEIVED. A COMEDY PERFORMED AT SIENA IN 1531: AND AELIA LAELIA CRISPIS (1862). *Drama.*
A BILL FOR THE BETTER PROMOTION OF OPPRESSION ON THE SABBATH DAY (1926). *Verse*
—privately printed.

Some Biographical and Critical Works:
THE LIFE OF THOMAS LOVE PEACOCK, by C. Van Doren (1911).
THOMAS LOVE PEACOCK. A CRITICAL STUDY, by A. M. Freeman (1911).
THOMAS LOVE PEACOCK, by J. B. Priestley (1927)
—in the English Men of Letters series.
MEREDITH AND PEACOCK. A STUDY IN LITERARY INFLUENCE, by A. H. Able. Philadelphia (1933).
PEACOCK, by O. W. Campbell (1953).

WRITERS AND THEIR WORK

General Editor: BONAMY DOBRÉE

The first 55 issues in the Series appeared under the General Editorship of T. O. BEACHCROFT

Sixteenth Century and Earlier:
FRANCIS BACON: J. Max Patrick
CHAUCER: Nevill Coghill
THE ENGLISH BIBLE: Donald Coggan
ENGLISH MARITIME WRITING:
    Hakluyt to Cook: Oliver Warner
MALORY: M. C. Bradbrook
MARLOWE: Philip Henderson
SIDNEY: Kenneth Muir
SKELTON: Peter Green
SPENSER: Rosemary Freeman
WYATT: Sergio Baldi

Seventeenth Century:
SIR THOMAS BROWNE: Peter Green
BUNYAN: Henri Talon
CAVALIER POETS: Robin Skelton
DONNE: Frank Kermode
DRYDEN: Bonamy Dobrée
HERBERT: T. S. Eliot
HERRICK: John Press
HOBBES: T. E. Jessop
BEN JONSON: J. B. Bamborough
LOCKE: Maurice Cranston
ANDREW MARVELL: John Press
MILTON: E. M. W. Tillyard
SHAKESPEARE: C. J. Sisson
  CHRONICLES: Clifford Leech
  EARLY COMEDIES: Derek Traversi
  FINAL PLAYS: F. Kermode
  GREAT TRAGEDIES: Kenneth Muir
  HISTORIES: L. C. Knights
  LATE COMEDIES: G. K. Hunter
  PROBLEM PLAYS: Peter Ure
THREE METAPHYSICAL POETS:
                Margaret Willy
IZAAK WALTON: Margaret Bottrall

Eighteenth Century:
BERKELEY: T. E. Jessop
BLAKE: Kathleen Raine
BOSWELL: P. A. W. Collins
BURKE: T. E. Utley
BURNS: David Daiches

COWPER: N. Nicholson
CRABBE: R. L. Brett
DEFOE: J. R. Sutherland
ENGLISH HYMNS: Arthur Pollard
FIELDING: John Butt
GIBBON: C. V. Wedgwood
GOLDSMITH: A. Norman Jeffares
GRAY: R. W. Ketton-Cremer
JOHNSON: S. C. Roberts
POPE: Ian Jack
RICHARDSON: R. F. Brissenden
SHERIDAN: W. A. Darlington
SMART: Geoffrey Grigson
SMOLLETT: Laurence Brander
STEELE, ADDISON AND THEIR
  PERIODICAL ESSAYS:
              A. R. Humphreys
STERNE: D. W. Jefferson
SWIFT: J. Middleton Murry
HORACE WALPOLE: Hugh Honour

Nineteenth Century:
MATTHEW ARNOLD: Kenneth Allott
JANE AUSTEN: S. Townsend Warner
THE BRONTË SISTERS: P. Bentley
BROWNING: John Bryson
SAMUEL BUTLER: G. D. H. Cole
BYRON: Herbert Read
CARLYLE: David Gascoyne
LEWIS CARROLL: Derek Hudson
CLOUGH: Isobel Armstrong
COLERIDGE: Kathleen Raine
DICKENS: K. J. Fielding
DISRAELI: Paul Bloomfield
GEORGE ELIOT: Lettice Cooper
ENGLISH TRAVELLERS IN THE NEAR
  EAST: Robin Fedden
FITZGERALD: Joanna Richardson
MRS. GASKELL: Miriam Allott
GISSING: A. C. Ward
THOMAS HARDY: R. A. Scott-James
HAZLITT: J. B. Priestley
G. M. HOPKINS: Geoffrey Grigson

T. H. HUXLEY: William Irvine
KEATS: Edmund Blunden
LAMB: Edmund Blunden
LANDOR: G. Rostrevor Hamilton
MACAULAY: G. R. Potter
JOHN STUART MILL: M. Cranston
WILLIAM MORRIS: P. Henderson
NEWMAN: J. M. Cameron
PATER: Iain Fletcher
ROSSETTI: Oswald Doughty
RUSKIN: Peter Quennell
SIR WALTER SCOTT: Ian Jack
SHELLEY: Stephen Spender
R. L. STEVENSON: G. B. Stern
SWINBURNE: H. J. C. Grierson
TENNYSON: F. L. Lucas
THACKERAY: Laurence Brander
FRANCIS THOMPSON: P. Butter
TROLLOPE: Hugh Sykes Davies
OSCAR WILDE: James Laver
WORDSWORTH: Helen Darbishire

Twentieth Century:

W. H. AUDEN: Richard Hoggart
HILAIRE BELLOC: Renée Haynes
ARNOLD BENNETT: F. Swinnerton
EDMUND BLUNDEN: Alec M. Hardie
ELIZABETH BOWEN: Jocelyn Brooke
ROBERT BRIDGES: John Sparrow
ROY CAMPBELL: David Wright
JOYCE CARY: Walter Allen
G. K. CHESTERTON: C. Hollis
WINSTON CHURCHILL: John Connell
R. G. COLLINGWOOD: E.W.F.Tomlin
I. COMPTON-BURNETT:
            Pamela Hansford Johnson
JOSEPH CONRAD: Oliver Warner
WALTER DE LA MARE: K. Hopkins
THE DETECTIVE STORY: J. Symons
NORMAN DOUGLAS: Ian Greenlees
T. S. ELIOT: M. C. Bradbrook
ENGLISH TRANSLATORS AND
      TRANSLATIONS: J. M. Cohen
RONALD FIRBANK and JOHN
        BETJEMAN: Jocelyn Brooke

FORD MADOX FORD: Kenneth Young
E. M. FORSTER: Rex Warner
CHRISTOPHER FRY: Derek Stanford
JOHN GALSWORTHY: R. H. Mottram
ROBERT GRAVES: M. Seymour Smith
GRAHAM GREENE: Francis Wyndham
L. P. HARTLEY and ANTHONY POW-
    ELL: P. Bloomfield and B. Bergonzi
A. E. HOUSMAN: Ian Scott-Kilvert
ALDOUS HUXLEY: Jocelyn Brooke
HENRY JAMES: Michael Swan
JAMES JOYCE: J. I. M. Stewart
RUDYARD KIPLING: B. Dobrée
D. H. LAWRENCE: Kenneth Young
C. DAY LEWIS: Clifford Dyment
WYNDHAM LEWIS: E. W. F. Tomlin
KATHERINE MANSFIELD: Ian Gordon
JOHN MASEFIELD: L. A. G. Strong
SOMERSET MAUGHAM: J. Brophy
EDWIN MUIR: J. C. Hall
J. MIDDLETON MURRY: Philip Mairet
GEORGE ORWELL: Tom Hopkinson
POETS OF THE 1939-45 WAR:
                        R. N. Currey
THE POWYS BROTHERS:
                        R. C. Churchill
J. B. PRIESTLEY: Ivor Brown
HERBERT READ: Francis Berry
BERTRAND RUSSELL: Alan Dorward
BERNARD SHAW: A. C. Ward
EDITH SITWELL: John Lehmann
OSBERT SITWELL: Roger Fulford
C. P. SNOW: William Cooper
STRACHEY: R. A. Scott-James
J. M. SYNGE and LADY GREGORY:
                    Elizabeth Coxhead
DYLAN THOMAS: G. S. Fraser
G. M. TREVELYAN: J. H. Plumb
WAR POETS: 1914-18: E. Blunden
EVELYN WAUGH: Christopher Hollis
H. G. WELLS: Montgomery Belgion
CHARLES WILLIAMS: Heath-Stubbs
VIRGINIA WOOLF: Bernard Blackstone
W. B. YEATS: G. S. Fraser

Forthcoming:

ENGLISH SERMONS: A. Pollard

HOOD: Laurence Brander